Training That Works
A Guide to On-the-Job Training

Charles M. Cadwell

American Media Publishing

4900 University Avenue
West Des Moines, IA 50266-6769
1-800-262-2557

Training That Works!
A Guide to On-the-Job Training

Charles M. Cadwell
Copyright ©1995 by American Media Incorporated

Credits:

American Media Publishing:	Arthur Bauer
	Todd McDonald
	Esther Vanier
Project Manager:	Leigh Lewis
Editor:	Bonnie G. Sanford
Designer:	Janet Ferguson Dooley

Published by American Media Inc., 4900 University Avenue, West Des Moines, IA 50266-6769
First Edition

Library of Congress Catalog Card Number 95-75606
Cadwell, Charles M.
Training That Works!
A Guide to On-the-Job Training

Printed in the United States of America
ISBN 1-884926-36-3

Introduction

On-the-job training. It's a training method used more frequently than any other. When you tell an employee how to do something, there is an assumption that it's on-the-job training. While there may be "training," there may be very little "learning." However, if the employee doesn't learn, the employee hasn't been trained.

Perhaps you are considering whether on-the-job training is appropriate for employees in your organization. Maybe you have been given the responsibility of training others but don't have a plan for how it should be accomplished. Whatever your position, this book will help. It provides guidelines for planning and conducting on-the-job training through the four-step training method, a proven system, as well as several tools to assist an organization and the trainer. And you'll find numerous examples of tried-and-tested approaches that will guarantee success with on-the-job training.

About the Author

Charles M. Cadwell is the President of Training Systems +, a company based in Kansas that specializes in training systems design and development. He has 20 years of experience in the training field.

Before starting Training Systems + in 1986, Mr. Cadwell held positions as Director of Field Training for Pizza Hut, Inc. and Director of Training for Popingo Video. He has worked with numerous Fortune 500 companies, as well as with many small- and medium-sized companies, to develop and conduct on-the-job training.

Mr. Cadwell is the author of several books and audio-cassette programs on the subjects of recruiting and selection, orientation and training, first-line supervision, coaching, empowerment, and leadership. His book, *The Human Touch Performance Appraisal,* was published in 1994 by American Media Publishing.

Acknowledgments

The author wishes to thank Mark Neeley, independent business consultant, and Todd McDonald at American Media Incorporated for their valuable contributions to this book.

TABLE OF CONTENTS

Chapter Six

Step Three — Tryout

Chapter Seven

Step Four — Follow-up

Chapter Eight

How to Handle Difficult Training Situations

Chapter Nine

Tools for Implementing On-the-Job Training and Evaluation

Answers to Chapter Exercises

CHAPTER ONE

A Brief Look at Why an Organization Should Train

Chapter Objectives

After reading this chapter and completing the interactive exercises, you should be able to:

 Describe the reasons for training.

 List the benefits of training to employees and to an organization.

☑ Describe what happens when training is done for the wrong reasons.

The Purpose of Training

There are two reasons for training:

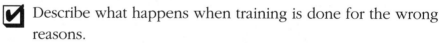 **1** **To teach job skills and behaviors.** Employees have to be taught skills and behaviors so they can perform their jobs. For example, a company purchases new equipment and the employees do not know how to use it, or an organization wants the employees to follow a different customer service process. In both, training is required.

To improve employee performance. An employee's performance may be declining because the correct method for accomplishing a task has been forgotten. For example, a retail company conducts an inventory at the end of every year. Even though the employees have done it before, a year has passed since the last inventory, so employees require a training session to review new procedures and be certain they understand their roles and responsibilities.

Take a Moment...

Take a moment to answer the following questions:

What skills and behaviors do your employees need that require training?

_____

_____

_____

_____

In what areas would training improve the performance of your employees?

_____

_____

_____

_____

How Do Employees and Organizations Benefit from Training?

Effective training will produce many benefits for employees and organizations:

The Employees

- **Greater job satisfaction.** Employees take more satisfaction in a job when they know how to do it well. If they aren't sure what to do or how to do it properly, they can be frustrated and dissatisfied with their work.

- **Peer acceptance.** Most employees want to be accepted as part of the work group. Learning a job quickly and being able to "pull their own weight" is one of the best ways for them to gain acceptance.

- **Improved self-esteem.** The combination of job satisfaction and peer acceptance lead to improved self-esteem.

- **Opportunity to advance in the organization.** Employees who demonstrate excellent performance at one level in an organization often have the opportunity to advance to other levels of responsibility.

- **Potential for greater earnings.** Advancement offers the potential for greater earnings.

The Organization

- **Increased productivity.** Employees who know how to perform their jobs are more effective and more productive than those who learn through trial and error.

- **Higher levels of customer satisfaction.** Employees are able to take care of customers properly and have better skills for solving customer-related problems.

- **Improved quality.** Standards are met when people know what the organization expects from them.

> *Is your organization taking advantage of all of these benefits?*

When Is Training Appropriate, and When Is It Not?

If a company is introducing a new telephone system, training would be required to teach employees how to use the system in the most productive manner. Training is not the answer when people already know what to do or there is an easier way to provide the necessary information. If employees know how to use the telephone system, but the company wants them to answer with a different greeting, sending a memo would be just as effective as a training session—and cost a lot less.

1

"Training is not the answer when people already know what to do or there is an easier way to provide the necessary information."

"80 percent of the problems employees have at work could be resolved by management following up on training."

Some Words of Caution

Employees may start taking shortcuts or making mistakes on the job without realizing they are doing so. In many of these situations, organizations spend hundreds of hours and even more dollars doing "refresher" training because they believe the employees have forgotten how to do a task. In reality, the problem often is with management. It's not that the employees don't know how to do the job, it's that they may not see the reasons for doing it the way management wants it done. It's been estimated that 80 percent of the problems employees have at work could be resolved by management following up on training and providing feedback to the employees.

In some companies, training is done because management believes it has to:

■ Reward the employees for their past efforts.

■ Fulfill legal obligations.

■ Show that the company is "doing something."

■ Follow the request of someone who says, "We need a training program."

When training is done for one of these reasons, time and money are invested poorly. Tangible results are not achieved, and there are no measurable benefits. In short, companies would be better off not training the employees.

Chapter One Review

Are the statements below True or False? Answers appear on page 96.

_____ 1. One reason for training is to improve behaviors.

_____ 2. Training would be helpful when learning how to operate a new computer system.

_____ 3. Employees' opportunities for advancement can be improved by training.

_____ 4. While learning a new job, employees rarely are concerned about being accepted by their co-workers.

_____ 5. Employees increase their earning potential when they are trained.

_____ 6. Effective training can produce higher levels of customer satisfaction.

_____ 7. If employees know how to perform a job satisfactorily, training should be conducted so they will think the organization cares about them.

1

Developing a Training Plan

Chapter Objectives

After reading this chapter and completing the interactive exercises, you should be able to:

☑ Write learning objectives.

☑ List the materials needed for the training.

☑ Prepare a training outline.

☑ Describe specific tryout and follow-up activities.

What is a Training Plan?

Effective on-the-job training requires a well-developed training plan. The plan may be prepared by the trainer or by anyone in the organization who has a thorough knowledge of the subject to be taught. It should be based on the four-step training method and should provide the trainer with the information necessary to complete all the steps successfully.

A well-developed training plan should include:
- Learning objectives.
- A list of training materials.
- An outline for the trainer to follow.
- Descriptions of the tryout and follow-up requirements.

"Effective on-the-job training requires a well-developed training plan."

On-the-Job Training Is Needed

Let's assume you have been asked to handle the on-the-job training for a new retail sales clerk. You know how to do the job, but how do you explain it to others? By developing an effective training plan.

Part of a sample training plan for a customer service representative is shown below. Notice that even though the "tryout" and "follow-up" steps are combined in this plan, it is organized according to the four-step method. That is because, in this case, the trainer will follow up immediately on what the trainee is trying out. However, there are different actions required by the trainer during the tryout and follow-up steps; therefore all four steps must be included.

Sample Customer Service Representative Training Plan Outline

I. Preparation

A. Learning Objectives

After training the employee will be able to:

- Answer the telephone correctly.
- Greet customers and welcome them to the store.

B. Materials Needed

- Operations Manual
- Telephone Job Aid
- Store Layout Diagram

II. Presentation/Demonstration

A. Answer the telephone correctly.

Explain how answering the phone affects customer perception.

- Employee attitude
- Answer within three rings
- What to say
- Voice inflection
- Routing calls to other departments
- Using the intercom
- What to do if you can't help the customer
- Handling upset customers

Using the trouble-shooting guide in the manual, summarize the key points of telephone procedure.

B. Greet customers and welcome them to the store.

III. Tryout/Follow-up

Employee tries the tasks listed below. Trainer follows up, as necessary, to ensure performance meets standards. Check each item as it is completed.

_____ Answering the telephone
_____ Routing calls to other departments
_____ Using the intercom
_____ Handling upset customers

Learning Objectives

To prepare an effective training plan, a trainer must first define the learning objectives. The choice of words is important. Note that these are learning objectives, not training objectives. You don't train to meet objectives. You train so employees will gain knowledge and will learn skills or behaviors that help them perform their jobs. The objectives should make it clear what the employees are expected to learn.

The best way to develop learning objectives is to complete the statement, "After training, the employee will be able to...." Give a clear description of what you want the trainees to do after completing the training.

Learning objectives must meet four criteria. They must be:

 Specific. The trainer should be clear about what is to be done during training.

 Measurable. The trainer should be able to measure the results.

 Realistic. The employee should be able to accomplish the task during training.

 Observable. The trainer should be able to see the trainee do it.

Do the following sample objectives meet the four criteria?
- Provide faster service.
- List the four-step method for on-the-job training.

2

Provide faster service has a nice ring to it, but the service is not specific and "faster" is not defined. That means it can't be measured. If it can't be measured, we don't know if it's realistic; therefore it can't be observed. Here's how the objective could be modified to fit the four criteria: **"To provide faster service, answer all incoming customer telephone calls within three rings."** Now there is a specific type of service (the telephone) that can be measured (within three rings to provide faster service). This is realistic and will tell the trainer if there are enough people to answer the telephone within three rings.

List the four-step method for on-the-job training meets all the criteria. This learning objective is specific (by requesting that the four-step method be listed) and measurable (the steps can be written). It's realistic (the trainee can perform the task), and it can be observed (when the task is performed).

"Doing" Words

Certain words should be used at the beginning of learning objectives to ensure that the objectives describe actions that are observable. They're called "doing" words. A few are listed below. You'll find more words in the section on writing learning objectives on page 87 of Chapter Nine.

List	**Write**
Name	**Demonstrate**
Describe	**Explain**
Perform	**Prepare**

Here are some **_words to avoid_** because the actions are vague:

Appreciate	**Know**
Understand	**Realize**

What does it look like when someone "appreciates" something? How do trainees "understand" something?

Take a Moment...

Developing objectives is the first step in preparing an on-the-job training plan. What should your employees be able to do after they are trained? List the objectives below. Start by thinking, "After training, my employees will be able to...."

_____

_____

_____

_____

Is each objective specific, measurable, realistic, and observable? If not, try rewriting it.

_____

_____

_____

_____

2

List of Training Materials

The next part of the training plan is a list of the training materials you'll need to meet your learning objectives during on-the-job training. You may not be able to complete the list until after the training outline has been prepared. So, start on the list after you have defined your learning objectives, but go back to it after the outline is finished to make sure you have included all the materials you'll need.

Four types of materials are used during training.

1 **Equipment and Tools**
- Rivet gun
- Flat-head screwdriver
- Open-end wrench
- Drill press
- Computer
- Calculator

2 **Trainer's Materials**
- Flip chart pad & markers
- White board & markers
- Audio tapes & equipment
- Video tapes & equipment
- Operations manuals
- Wall charts

3 **Reference Materials**
- Operations Manual
- Policies and Procedures
- Manufacturers' manuals
- Blueprints
- Technical specifications
- Safety goggles

4 **Employee's Materials**
- Workbooks or paper for taking notes
- Pens or pencils
- Handouts
- Sample finished products

The types of materials will vary based on the type of training and the location of the training. If the training requires many materials, you'll find it helpful to divide the list into the four categories. However, if you have only a few items, you may wish to use one list.

"The types of materials will vary based on the type of training and the location of the training."

18

Take a Moment...

What materials will you need for on-the-job training? List them below.

Equipment and Tools

_____
_____
_____
_____

Reference Materials

_____
_____
_____
_____

Trainer's Materials

_____
_____
_____
_____

Employee's Materials

_____
_____
_____
_____

2

The Training Outline

Learning objectives tell you where you need to go. The training outline tells you how to get there. It's your road map for guiding participants.

The training outline is a plan for how you will present and demonstrate the task to convey the learning objectives. The amount of detail in this outline will depend on the complexity of the task being taught. If you are developing the outline for yourself, it may be brief. If you are developing the outline for other trainers who are not as familiar with the topic, or the subject to be taught is complex, you will need more detail. As you are working on your outline, refer to the **Training Outline Template**[1] on page 88 in Chapter Nine.

The learning objectives should serve as your guide when developing the outline. Ideally, each objective will have a corresponding section in the training outline. Look back at the objectives in the sample training outline for customer service training on page 13.

You probably noticed that the outline was not completed for the second learning objective, "Greet customers and welcome them to the store." Based on your knowledge of customer service (you're a customer), write the activities below that will be needed to meet the second objective. Be specific, but don't go into too much detail or the outline will be hard to use.

The telephone portion of the customer service outline lists the key activities to be performed, but also includes a look at the company's trouble-shooting guide. The trainer should be familiar with the company's manual.

Greet and welcome customers to the store.

_____

_____

1Reprinted by permission of publisher, from *Developing an Employee Orientation and Training Program* by Charles M. Cadwell, 1990, American Management Association. All rights reserved.

The Whole-Part-Whole Approach

Use the whole-part-whole approach when developing the outline. Begin with an overview (whole) of the job to be trained and explain why it is important. Next, present and demonstrate each step (part) of the training. Summarize by pulling all the parts back together (whole). Take another look at the customer service outline. List the whole-part-whole descriptions below. List only the first two items for the "part."

Whole:

_____

_____

_____

Part:

_____

_____

_____

Whole:

_____

_____

_____

Did you find them? The first whole is "Explain how answering the phone affects customer perception." The first two items in the part section are "Employee attitude" and "Answer within three rings." The second whole is "Summarize the key points of telephone procedure."

The whole-part-whole approach to training follows the saying, "Tell them what you're going to tell them (whole), tell them (part), and then tell them what you told them (whole)." Using this approach will keep you focused when you are developing the outline and when you are conducting the on-the-job training.

21

Take a Moment...

Consider one of the learning objectives for your training plan.

What is the "whole" at the beginning?

_____

_____

List the first two "parts" of your training outline.

_____

_____

What is the "whole" for summarizing the objective?

_____

_____

Tryout and Follow-up Activities

Often a trainer does not ask trainees to perform the task being demonstrated. The trainees' understanding of the task will not be complete unless they "try" the tasks being demonstrated and the trainer "follows up."

Trainers should refer to the learning objectives when defining what the trainees will practice.

In the customer service outline, the employee is required to perform the following tasks to "answer the telephone correctly":

_____ Answering the telephone
_____ Routing calls to other departments
_____ Using the intercom
_____ Handling upset customers

"Trainers should refer to the learning objectives when defining what the trainees will practice."

The items are in a checklist format so that when a trainee performs to the standard, the trainer may either initial or place a check mark on the line. This serves two purposes: It provides the trainee with positive reinforcement that a task has been learned and enables the trainer to keep track of the trainee's progress.

Your organization may elect to use the outline as documentation that training was conducted and that the trainee learned the task. If so, a signatures block similar to the following may be added at the end of the follow-up section:

The signatures below indicate that the trainee has satisfactorily completed the training outlined above according to standards established by the trainer and the company.

_____   _____

      Employee Signature   *Date*

_____   _____

      Trainer Signature   *Date*

This signature block also serves as a double-check on the training process. The signed outline is filed in a permanent place, such as the employee's personnel record, to verify that training was completed.

Take a Moment...

Consider one of the learning objectives of your training plan. What do you want the trainees to practice during tryout?

_____

_____

_____

_____

Chapter Two Review

Complete each of the following statements and questions. Suggested answers appear on page 96.

1. Well-written learning objectives should meet what four criteria?

   _____

   _____

   _____

   _____

2. Rewrite the following objective so it meets the four criteria:
   "Increase sales over last year."

   _____

   _____

3. What two types of equipment might be included in a list of materials for an on-the-job training session?

   _____

   _____

4. Read the following statements. Check all that are TRUE.

   _____ The training outline is like a road map.
   _____ Other resources may be used to supplement the outline.
   _____ The training outline should follow the part-whole approach.
   _____ The training outline should list key points for the trainer to try out.

5. The analogy for a training outline is:

Whole _____

_____ Tell them _____

Whole _____

6. Tryout is only necessary when there is a short presentation.
   _____ True
   _____ False

7. A signature block often is used at the end of a training outline for the following reasons: (Check all that are TRUE.)

   _____ To make sure the employee shows up for training
   _____ Document that the trainer did the training
   _____ Verify that the employee learned the material

8. Effective trainers only use training outlines the first time they conduct a training session.
   _____ True
   _____ False

2

CHAPTER THREE

The Four-Step Training Method for On-the-Job Training

Chapter Objectives

After reading this chapter and completing the interactive exercises, you should be able to:

 Describe the four-step training method.

 List the benefits of the four-step method.

 Explain when the four-step method should be used.

 List the barriers that must be overcome so you will be successful with the four-step method.

History of the Four-Step Training Method

The four-step training method was introduced in this country by the military during World War II when there was a need to train a large number of people quickly and effectively. Since that time, thousands of businesses and nonprofit organizations have adopted the four-step method as the preferred method for on-the-job training.

Here is a summary of the four-step method. The steps will be discussed in detail in Chapters Four through Seven.

The Four-Step Training Method Outline

I. Preparation

- Prepare yourself (the trainer)
- Prepare training materials
- Prepare training environment
- Prepare trainees

II. Presentation/Demonstration

- Present training content
- Demonstrate task
- Verify trainees understand task

III. Tryout

- Implement trainees' practice
- Observe trainees' practice
- Provide feedback to trainees
- Help trainees gain speed and develop accuracy

IV. Follow-up

- Have trainees work alone
- Designate "helpers" for trainees
- Reconfirm trainees understand task
- Evaluate training procedures

Some companies have made a few modifications and use either a three-step or a five-step method. Usually, the three-step method combines the tryout and follow-up steps (as shown in the Sample Customer Service Representative Training Plan Outline on page 13 in Chapter Two). Another three-step modification links the presentation/demonstration with the tryout.

Benefits of Four-Step Training

There are several benefits to using the four-step method. Let's review them below:

- It's easy to understand and to use. Using the four-step outline will ensure a satisfying training experience for everyone.
- It can be used on the job. It doesn't need a classroom or special equipment, other than what would be required for the workplace.
- It doesn't require training expertise to use it. Almost anyone who has the desire and willingness to become a trainer will achieve success with this method.
- It provides a template for any training situation. The trainer decides what is important based upon the training situation and makes changes when necessary.

> *One of the best things about the four-step method is its universal application.*
>
> *Even if the trainer has very little training experience, the four-step method allows procedures to be explained in the simplest terms.*

When Should the Four-Step Method Be Used?

Many organizations hold "school" to "teach" lessons to their "students." **Classroom instruction may be beneficial in some on-the-job training situations, but in many others, the four-step method is more appropriate and more cost-effective.** Here are a few examples of when the four-step method should be used:

- **Time Constraints.** A company hires a new employee who has to be able to begin working immediately. The employee can't wait for a training class to be scheduled. Another company has a procedure change which must be implemented quickly. It affects a group of employees, but there is not enough time to arrange classroom training. Both companies would benefit from the four-step training method.

- **Line Management Training Responsibility.** In some cases, line management employees are the only people who know the job well enough to train other employees. They may not have the time or the inclination to develop the skills to conduct formal classroom training. Also they may not be comfortable in front of large groups but do work well with small groups or in a one-on-one setting.

- **Workplace Flexibility.** It may be too expensive to purchase equipment, supplies, or materials for the classroom. The four-step method can be used in the workplace where everything is available. Training also can be combined with other responsibilities so the employee is not away from the work area.

3

- **Cost Considerations.** When employees are sent to a classroom training session, the company either has to replace them temporarily in the workplace or has to give up their productivity. Four-step on-the-job training also eliminates, or reduces, the costs of transportation, lodging, food, and other expenses that often are associated with classroom training.

- **Realistic Setting.** Training is more effective when learning takes place in the "real world," rather than in a simulated environment. When the training occurs at an off-site location, employees may have more difficulty using their skills on the job.

Take a Moment...

Does your organization have on-the-job training requirements that would benefit from the four-step method? Consider these factors:

Time Constraints _____

_____

Line Management Training Responsibility _____

_____

Workplace Flexibility _____

_____

Cost Considerations _____

_____

Realistic Setting _____

_____

Breaking the Barriers to Successful On-the-Job Training

While there are many advantages to using the four-step method, problems could arise which would present barriers to successful on-the-job training.

Training Barrier 1

Wrong Trainer

The Problem. Even though your company selected a person with a lot of training experience, that person did not provide the best training for the employees.

The Solution. A trainer does not have to be an expert. There are a few qualities an effective trainer must possess, though.

- **Good Communication Skills.** Effective trainers have to be clear and concise in their training and must specify what is expected from the trainees. They also need good listening skills that enable them to be "in tune" with what the trainees are saying. Providing feedback is another important communication skill. Trainees want to know when they are doing the job properly or when corrective action is required.

- **Knowledge of the Subject.** An in-depth knowledge of the subject is critical when using the four-step method. The trainer must have a comprehensive understanding of the job to be able to fill in the details of the training outline.

3

- **On-the-Job Experience.** An effective trainer has done the task several times before and understands what it takes to do it successfully. The knowledge and skills acquired over time provide special insights that can be passed on to the trainees. This is important, especially when a new procedure is being introduced.

- **Patience.** Learning a task can be frustrating for the trainee. When the trainee has difficulty, it also can be frustrating for the trainer. Having patience when others make mistakes is a real virtue. Unfortunately, some trainers cannot understand why employees do not learn tasks quickly.

- **Interest in Helping People Learn.** People who train others because "they have to" or "didn't have a choice" do not make effective trainers. The best trainers are those who enjoy working with others and have a sense of achievement when they see someone learning a new skill. Successful trainers take as much, if not more, pride in the accomplishment of their trainees as in their ability to train.

- **Respect of Others.** It is important that other employees respect the knowledge and skills of the person who is assigned to do the training. This respect becomes doubly important when a new skill is being taught. Trainees must have confidence in the ability of their trainer.

- **Sense of Humor.** Having a sense of humor means more than just telling stories. When faced with learning something new, many trainees feel under pressure to learn quickly without making any mistakes. A trainer with a sense of humor can put people at ease by not reacting in anger when something goes wrong and by letting them know it's not the end of the world if they have trouble learning a new task.

Take a Moment...

Who in your organization would make effective on-the-job trainers? List their names and special qualities below. Consider these factors:

Good Communication Skills _____

_____

Knowledge of Subject _____

_____

Experience _____

_____

Patience _____

_____

Interest in Helping People Learn _____

_____

Respect of Others _____

_____

Sense of Humor _____

_____

Training Barrier 2

Misperception of Time Required to Conduct Training

The Problem. Your employees may be reluctant to become trainers because they think it will require a great amount of time to prepare and present the information and to complete the follow-up.

The Solution. Emphasize to employees who may be potential trainers that:

- A well-developed outline based upon the four-step method will save time by providing all the necessary "prompts."

- The first on-the-job training session involves the most preparation time. Preparation should decrease as the number of training presentations increases.

- After-the-training follow-up will be done during the trainee's working hours. If the training necessitates "add-on" or after-hours time, days off or salary compensation will be offered.

Take a Moment...

What time barriers exist in your organization that would affect potential trainers? List them below, along with what can be done to remove the barriers.

Time Barrier	Ways to Remove the Barrier
_____	_____
_____	_____
_____	_____
_____	_____

Training Barrier 3

Lack of Trainee Motivation

The Problem. Your trainers have had situations when the trainees aren't motivated by what they are being taught.

The Solution. It is important to find a way to motivate the trainee so that it benefits both the trainee and the company. The trainer should remember that:

- Trainees may not see the importance of training as it relates to the job. Here's an example of how to emphasize why trainees should be motivated: *Learning preventive maintenance on equipment may seem unnecessary, but not doing so could lead to downtime and a reduction in employee hours.*

- If the trainee is not enthusiastic about a task because it is routine or repetitive, the trainer should be straightforward rather than trying to create an illusion of excitement. It should be stressed that every task is integral to the overall performance of the job.

- Creative, constructive ways must be found to change the trainee's attitude. A positive focus on why training is being given and the importance of the training to the employees and to the company will improve the training process.

"It should be stressed that every task is integral to the overall performance of the job."

Take a Moment...

What trainee motivation barriers exist in your organization that might affect the success of on-the-job training efforts? List them below, along with what should be done to remove the barriers.

Motivation Barrier	Ways to Remove the Barrier
_____	_____
_____	_____
_____	_____

Chapter Three Review

Fill in the blanks for each of the following statements. Suggested answers appear on page 97.

1. The four-step training method sequence is:

   I. Preparation

   II. _____

   III. _____

   IV. Follow-up

2. List three benefits of using the four-step method for on-the-job training.

   _____

   _____

   _____

3. When should the four-step method be used?

   Time _____

   Line _____ Training Responsibility

   Workplace _____

   Cost _____

   Realistic _____

4. List at least five qualities of effective trainers:

    _____

    _____

    _____

    _____

    _____

5. The _____ on-the-job training session usually requires
    the most preparation time.

6. When the trainee is not enthusiastic, a trainer should keep a

    _____   _____

    on why training is being given.

3

Step One - Preparation

Chapter Objectives

After reading this chapter and completing the interactive exercises, you should be able to:

 Prepare yourself to conduct training.

 Prepare the training materials.

☑ Prepare the training environment.

☑ Prepare the trainees for the training.

The Key to Success

Preparation is the key to success with on-the-job training. By being prepared, the trainer creates a positive learning experience which makes trainees enthusiastic about learning the task.

The amount of time required for preparation will vary according to the complexity of the subject, the number of times the training has been conducted, and the type of training materials used. However, a solid training plan will reduce the preparation time.

> **"...a solid training plan will reduce the preparation time."**

The first step of the four-step training method is "preparation."

During this step you will:
- Prepare yourself (the trainer)
- Prepare training materials
- Prepare training environment
- Prepare trainees

Prepare Yourself

The time you invest preparing yourself for training will be returned to you several fold. More preparation is required for the first training presentation. It's likely the second session will take additional time, also, as you'll want to incorporate what you learned during the first training session and eliminate or reduce problems that occurred. By the third you'll be a pro!

Preparing yourself for training involves the following activities:

- **Reviewing the Content.** Once you have your training outline in hand, your first step will be to read the outline for flow and content. Be sure you can describe the whole-part-whole of the outline. What will you do first, second, and thereafter? If you have questions or want to add items, write them on the outline immediately. When you finish reading the outline, summarize the message of the training in a few words. Do you understand it?

  Next, if the outline is based on reference material, obtain the material and review it. This will answer some of your questions and give you additional ideas for the training. Finish preparing the content by reading the outline one more time. This will finalize the outline, and you'll be ready to move to the next activity.

- **Practicing the Training Presentation.** The idea of practicing for on-the-job training may seem to be preparation overkill, but it is time well-spent. New trainers often are amazed at what they say and do when it's "live" training. What sounds good in our heads just doesn't seem to come out of our mouths the same way!

The two best ways to practice are:

 Use a tape recorder. What you hear when you play the tape may surprise you.

 Ask one or two people to allow you to "train" them. Use people who don't know anything, or who know very little, about the task.

Continue practicing until you have confidence in yourself and your material. You may feel this way after the first practice, or it may take two or three times. Don't short-change your trainees by skipping this important step.

■ **Becoming Physically and Mentally "Ready."** Tomorrow you're conducting a training session. You've prepared the content and practiced it until you know the material forward and backward. You're ready to go—almost. Don't forget to prepare yourself physically and mentally for the training.

Here are ten techniques that will ensure your success:
1. Be rested.
2. Arrive early to solve any last-minute problems.
3. Limit food intake.
4. Avoid milk products and carbonated beverages. Drink water.
5. Limit caffeine intake.
6. Dress comfortably and appropriately.
7. Organize your materials.
8. Go to the restroom before you start training.
9. Think positive thoughts:
   I know the material.
   I have reviewed resource materials.
   I have practiced.
10. Remember that your trainees are there to learn, not to judge you.

Take a Moment...

List and explain the three activities that will prepare you for conducting on-the-job training.

1. _____

_____

2. _____

_____

3. _____

_____

4

Prepare the Training Materials

The materials needed for on-the-job training will depend on the subject being taught. If you added materials while you were practicing, be sure you've written them on your training outline. You may find it helpful to develop a separate materials checklist that can be photocopied. This allows you to check off the materials as they are gathered for each training session.

Here are some hints that will help you organize the materials:

- Know how many employees you are training.
- Have extra sets of materials, if needed, for the tryout or in case you have to train other employees at the last minute.
- Ensure that you have access to all the equipment and materials you will need.
- Put materials in the order in which you will use them and be sure they are accessible.
- Be sure you have an up-to-date copy of the materials.
- Take along reference materials and manuals to answer specific questions.

- Have examples of the finished product or job available so the employees can see what they are expected to do.
- Be sure power sources are available for equipment.
- Have pens or pencils available.
- Have safety gear available.
- Verify that computer programs are up and running.

When conducting several training sessions, it may be more economical to photocopy the materials for all of the sessions at one time, rather than copying them whenever you offer the training. If so, find a place where you can store the materials between training sessions.

Take a Moment...

List how you will prepare the training materials for your on-the-job training session.

_____

_____

_____

_____

"Trainees develop good work habits when they learn in the proper environment."

Prepare the Training Environment

Trainees develop good work habits when they learn in the proper environment. Trainers who ask participants for feedback often are surprised that the environment gets more critical comments than any other part of the training. The room was too hot or too cold, or the lights were too bright or too dim, or the training area was messy, or the trainer could not be seen during the presentation and demonstration. Preparing the training environment properly is a task that cannot be overlooked or taken for granted.

The best environment is one that isn't noticed. There is adequate space in which to learn and there are no distractions. If you're training in the workplace and not a classroom, you will have to adapt your plan to the environmental factors that are there.

How Does Your Environment Rate?

Is your training environment under control? Ask yourself the following questions:

- Is the work area as clean and neat as possible?
- Has all the trash been removed?
- Have items that are not related to the training been put away?
- Is the air temperature and ventilation acceptable?
- Is there adequate lighting?
- Are tables or chairs available?
- Are training materials accessible?
- Have telephone calls been diverted?
- Is there a "Quiet, Please. Training in Progress." sign in place?
- Is the area free from distractions?
- Have safety precautions been taken?
- Are coffee or refreshments needed, and if so, are they available?

4

Take a Moment...

List the steps you will take to prepare the environment for your on-the-job training session.

_____

_____

_____

_____

Prepare the Trainees

Preparing employees for training begins the moment you meet. Put them at ease so they will be comfortable during the training.

Make sure that the trainees know your name and your position with the company. If you're certain the trainees already know you, then greet them as soon as you meet them. This is especially important if they are coming to an unfamiliar training location.

Consider the following ideas for making your trainees comfortable during on-the-job training:

- As the trainer, introduce yourself.
- If there is more than one trainee, have them introduce themselves.
- Cover the "necessities," such as restroom locations, breaks, food, drinks.
- Tell them *emergency* messages and telephone calls will be put through, but all others must be handled during breaks.
- Let them know the approximate length of the training session.
- Tell them the number of training sessions they must attend.
- Allow them to ask a few questions before the training begins.
- Review the learning objectives before the training begins and repeat during training.
- Communicate what you expect from them during the training.
- Keep the session informal by encouraging their questions and participation.

Take a Moment...

List the ways in which you will prepare trainees for your on-the-job training session.

_____

_____

_____

_____

Chapter Four Review

Are the statements below True or False? The answers appear on page 97.

_____ 1. Preparation time can be reduced by having a solid training plan.

_____ 2. The most preparation time will be required the first time you conduct the training.

_____ 3. Practicing your presentation is not necessary if you have previously done any type of training.

_____ 4. Drinking coffee with caffeine can help keep you alert during the training.

_____ 5. Thinking positive thoughts can help make your training go smoother.

_____ 6. A list of training materials should be included in the training outline.

_____ 7. The materials needed for on-the-job training will depend on the subject being taught.

_____ 8. Trainees often are more critical of the training environment than any other aspect of the training.

_____ 9. Trainees should be able to make calls and receive messages during training.

4

Step Two - Presentation/ Demonstration

Chapter Objectives

After reading this chapter and completing the interactive exercises, you should be able to:

 Present the training content.

 Demonstrate the task to the trainees.

 Verify that the trainees understand the task.

Show and Tell

Most of us had our first experiences with on-the-job training in grade school during "Show and Tell." The success of the four-step training method depends on how well the basic show-and-tell (presentation) principles are explained to the participants before they see the task demonstrated.

The second step of the four-step training method is "Presentation/Demonstration."

During this step you will:
- Present Training Content
- Demonstrate the Task
- Verify Trainees Understand Task

Present the Training Content

Keep in mind that the key points of your presentation and demonstration are based on the learning objectives of the training outline. Begin by telling the trainees the learning objectives for the session. If they know where you are leading them, they are likely to follow.

There are several techniques which you can follow that will make your presentation more effective.

- **Follow a Logical Sequence.** Explain the procedure in a step-by-step manner. Begin with the first thing to be done, followed by the second step, and so on.

- **Be Clear and Concise.** Get to the point and eliminate anything that's extraneous. The less you say, the less the trainees will have to remember.

- **Explain the Reasons "Why."** Giving an explanation of why it is best to perform the task a certain way will keep trainees from developing bad habits.

- **Stress Key Points.** Provide the key points and ensure the trainee is focused on learning the job.

- **Avoid Jargon and Buzz Words.** Keep your presentation simple and to the point. Too many terms will confuse the trainee.

- **Speak at a Moderate Speed.** Avoid speaking too slowly—you may offend the trainee. On the other hand, if you speak too quickly, the trainee may not be able to comprehend an idea before you move on to the next one.

"Begin by telling the trainees the learning objectives for the session."

5

■ **Make Frequent Eye Contact.** Look at your trainees frequently during the presentation. Maintain eye contact for approximately three to five seconds before you look away. The expressions in the trainees' eyes will offer clues as to how well they are understanding what you are saying.

■ **Be Enthusiastic.** Demonstrate your interest in the topic. If the trainees appear bored, they may be reflecting back the message you are sending them. Enthusiasm is contagious, and the participants will catch it.

Take a Moment...

Think about your on-the-job training session as you review the presentation techniques below. In the space provided, write a few actions that will improve your next presentation. You will find it helpful to mark the training outline where you want to take the action.

Presentation Techniques:
■ Follow a logical sequence.
■ Be clear and concise.
■ Explain the reasons "why."
■ Stress key points.
■ Avoid jargon and buzz words.
■ Speak at a moderate speed.
■ Make frequent eye contact.
■ Be enthusiastic.

Actions:

_____

_____

_____

_____

Demonstrate the Task

It has been estimated that people remember only 20 percent of what they hear but up to 50 percent of what they see and hear. So, it makes sense that you should demonstrate the task.

Here are several techniques that will make your demonstration more effective.

- **Position the Employee Correctly.** The trainee must be able to see the entire demonstration. If possible, avoid having the trainee opposite you, as this creates a mirror image, and the trainee has to sort out what is done with right and left hands. The best position is beside. Depending on the angle and the space available, you may have to step back occasionally or exaggerate your movements while performing the task.

- **Use Manageable Sections.** Demonstrate the task one step at a time. If possible, have the demonstration follow the sequence of your presentation. Presenting the whole task at one time will cause confusion and will overload the trainee with too much information.

- **Demonstrate First at the Expected Work Speed.** The first time you demonstrate the task, do it at the required speed. This will establish the standards for speed and accuracy. Do not try to impress the trainee by doing the task faster. Explain that you don't expect the trainee to achieve this same speed and accuracy immediately.

- **Demonstrate Next at a Slower Speed.** Although you may have done the job one hundred times, it's the first time for the trainee. A slower speed will enable the trainee to learn the task and grasp the details.

"It has been estimated that people remember only 20 percent of what they hear but up to 50 percent of what they see and hear."

5

■ **Use Real Materials, Props, or Cut-Aways.** Whenever possible, use real materials during the demonstration. If this is not possible, obtain or develop a prop. Request that your company provide samples, props, or cut-aways for the training. The more realistic the demonstration, the easier it is for the trainee to complete the tryout step.

Take a Moment...

Think about your on-the-job training session as you review the demonstration techniques below. In the space provided, write a few actions that will improve your next demonstration. You will find it helpful to mark the training outline where you want to take the action.

Demonstration Techniques:
■ Position the employee correctly.
■ Use manageable sections.
■ Demonstrate first at the expected work speed.
■ Demonstrate next at a slower speed.
■ Use real materials, props, or cutaways.

Actions:

_____

_____

_____

_____

Verify That Trainees Understand the Task

Even if you present and demonstrate a task the same way every time you train, it is unlikely that all trainees will respond in the same manner. Some will learn quicker than others, some will have more questions, and some, in spite of your best efforts, may never quite understand the task. It's important that you verify the trainee's understanding of the task before you move to the tryout step in the training process.

There are three ways you can test a trainee's understanding.

1 ▾ Ask for Questions.

At points throughout the training, ask trainees, "What questions do you have?" With this request, you are indicating that questions are part of the training process. Trainees are more likely to ask their own questions once they realize it is expected. Your request may be answered with a "No," if you ask, "Do you have any questions?" Trainees may not want to admit they have questions because they're afraid it will indicate they are incapable of comprehending the task. It also could mean they are confused.

You also can "prime" them by saying, "One of the questions I'm often asked is....," then answering the question yourself.

2 ▾ Have Trainees Repeat Instructions.

Focus on relevant points that must be followed to perform the task properly. Don't ask them to repeat the entire process. Tell them that you are asking them to repeat instructions because you are concerned about how well you communicated the message. You could say, "Just to be sure I was clear, tell me how you should...." This approach keeps the trainees from feeling threatened and allows them to respond with brief answers.

"It's important that you verify the trainee's understanding of the task before you move to the tryout step in the training process."

5

If the trainees repeat the instructions correctly, respond, "Good. I'm glad my instructions were clear." If they have difficulty, correct them in a constructive manner: "I may have forgot to mention that...." As the trainer, you have to assume responsibility for the accuracy of the communication.

3 ▼ Test Verbally for Understanding.

Keep the questions short and to the point. Your goal is to verify understanding while reinforcing what the trainees are learning. Usually you'll need only two or three questions to determine what the trainees have learned. This allows the trainees to develop the confidence that they are making progress and that they are learning the task.

Try to avoid questions which can be answered with a simple "Yes" or "No," as these answers give very little insight into what the trainees have learned. Ask open-ended questions that begin with words such as what, why, how, when, or where. For example, "Where would you store the oily rags after cleaning the equipment?"

Take a Moment...

Think about your on-the-job training session as you review the verification techniques below. In the space provided, write a few actions you can take to confirm that trainees understand the task. It is helpful to mark the training outline where you want to take these actions.

Verification Techniques:
- Ask for questions.
- Have trainees repeat instructions.
- Test verbally for understanding.

Actions:

_____

_____

_____

Chapter Five Review

Complete each of the following statements. Suggested answers appear on pages 97 and 98.

1. The third step of the four-step training method is similar to _____ and _____.

2. The key points of your presentation and demonstration are the _____ _____.

3. When explaining a procedure, your instructions should follow a _____ sequence.

4. Two things to avoid when making a presentation are _____ and _____ words.

5. Eye contact that lasts for _____ to _____ seconds helps you verify that the trainees are understanding your presentation.

6. The best place for the trainee to stand when you are demonstrating a task is _____.

7. The first time you demonstrate the task, do it at the _____speed.

8. When asking questions to verify understanding, it is best to avoid questions that can be answered by _____ or_____.

9. A good trainer accepts _____ for the accuracy of the instruction the trainee receives.

10. Speak slowly when making a presentation so the trainee will understand what you are saying.
    _____ True
    _____ False

11. The primary reason to have the trainee repeat instructions is to help you find out who is paying attention.
    _____ True
    _____ False

CHAPTER SIX

Step Three - Tryout

Chapter Objectives

After reading this chapter and completing the interactive exercises, you should be able to:

 Implement the trainees' practice.

 Observe the trainees' ability to do the task during practice.

 Provide feedback to the trainee.

✔ Help the trainee gain speed and develop accuracy.

Why a Tryout?

You've read in the section on demonstrating the task that it has been estimated that people retain up to 50 percent of what they see and hear. If trainees practice a task after it is presented and demonstrated to them, the estimate of what they will remember increases to 90 percent. That's the reason "tryout" follows the presentation/demonstration step in the four-step training method.

The third step of the four-step training method is "tryout."

During this step you will:

- Implement Trainees' Practice
- Observe Trainees' Practice
- Provide Feedback to Trainees
- Help Trainees Gain Speed and Develop Accuracy

Approaches to the Tryout Step

Experienced trainers take different approaches to the tryout step. Some keep it separate from the follow-up, while others prefer to have trainees perform them both at the same time. Trainers also have combined the tryout with the presentation and demonstration. You should decide which method will work best for you. That decision may be determined by the task being trained.

Inexperienced trainers often stop the training process after they've completed the presentation and demonstration. They assume that because they have "trained," surely the trainees have "learned." Unfortunately, that's not always the case. During practice the trainer will determine what trainees have learned, identify any problem areas, and help them increase their proficiency.

Never leave trainees to their own devices during the tryout. Rather, the trainer must be alert and involved in the continuing learning process.

Implement Trainees' Practice

A tryout should follow the presentation and demonstration as soon as it is practical. The less time that passes between the presentation/demonstration step and the practice, the easier it will be for the trainees to perform the task correctly. The trainees also will require less review.

To make the practice time beneficial:

- **Have the Trainees Explain the Task.** Their explanation will help you determine whether they understand what you've taught. If every trainee makes the same mistake, you'll want to assess the points at which the presentation and demonstration were not clear.

"Verbalizing the task while they are performing it also reinforces the trainees' understanding."

Verbalizing the task while they are performing it also reinforces the trainees' understanding. In a sense, they are "programming" their minds to recall the correct procedures. If their explanations are incomplete, correct them so they aren't "programmed" the wrong way.

■ **Ask the Trainees to Repeat the Practice to Create Habits.** It has been said that "Practice makes perfect." Well, it does, provided it is a perfect practice. Some trainees are able to practice the task correctly the first time, while others will have difficulty. Multiple practices are important because they create habits.

The number of times a task needs to be practiced will vary from trainee to trainee. The trainer can move on to another task after the trainee consecutively performs the task correctly two or three times.

Take a Moment...

Think about how you can ensure that the trainee's practice is beneficial during on-the-job training.

What tasks will you have the trainee repeat? Why?

_____

_____

_____

At what points will you have the trainee explain the task?

_____

_____

_____

Observe Trainees' Practice

Watch the trainees as they practice and note any areas which need to be clarified or corrected. The goal of practice is to give the trainees the opportunity to practice the task in a controlled environment while someone is available to help.

There are three ways to make the observation process easier:

 Assess how you observe. As you watch the trainees practice:

- **Explain why you are observing.** Tell the trainees you are verifying that the presentation and demonstration were sufficient for them to perform the task.

- **Look at individual steps.** Watch the steps in the process to determine which ones are correct and which need to be improved.

- **Review the task more than once.** Have the trainees perform the task two or three times to verify that they have the techniques and the knowledge required to work independently.

- **Evaluate the end result.** Does the product or performance meet the standard? What areas of the process created problems for the end result?

Recognize your influence on the trainees. Trainees often are nervous just because they are learning something new. With a trainer watching, they can feel pressured during practice. Trainees need to be assured that the trainer is not being critical of their mistakes. You can say, "If someone was watching me, it would make me nervous. Don't worry about making a mistake."

 Give the trainees breathing room. If you are working with small groups and you have some trainees who are learning quicker than others, have those who learn the task first assist the others who still need help. This approach allows trainees to work with their peers, who are less intimidating than a trainer. Allowing trainees to work with less direct observation from the trainer also can build their confidence because they will feel that you are beginning to trust their ability.

Take a Moment...

Think about how you will observe the trainees during on-the-job training.

What will be your focus while observing the practice?

_____

_____

What will you do to ensure the trainees don't feel intimidated?

_____

_____

What will you do to give them breathing room?

_____

_____

Provide Feedback to Trainees

Everyone wants feedback about how they perform. Trainees need even more because they are learning something new. Giving feedback to trainees during the tryout is very important. If you don't give this feedback, the trainees will assume they are right. Don't let them make assumptions, especially if they're wrong. Offer lots of feedback in the beginning, then taper off gradually. It's better to err on the side of giving too much feedback than not giving enough.

When giving feedback it should be:

- **Specific.** Tell the trainee exactly what you saw. Avoid vague and general statements.
- **Immediate.** Give feedback as soon as you see the trainees perform the task correctly or incorrectly. Don't wait for them to do it again.
- **Earned.** Avoid feedback that isn't deserved just to make the trainees feel good. Dishonest feedback is worse than no feedback at all.
- **Individualized.** Give feedback to each person, not just to the group as a whole. Using the trainees' names also individualizes them.
- **Positive.** Remember that feedback always should be positive, even when telling trainees they are practicing the task incorrectly.

Here are some ways to offer positive feedback:

- **Recognize successes.** Acknowledging successes provides reinforcement and lets the trainees know you are encouraged by what they are learning.
- **Correct mistakes in a supportive manner.** Most trainees will make errors. If they knew how to perform the task, they wouldn't need the training! Sometimes trainees become so concerned about errors that they make the same mistake over and over. Correct mistakes in a supportive manner by focusing on the task being performed, not on the person performing it.

> **"Giving feedback to trainees during the tryout is very important."**

6

59

Step In, When Necessary

There may be times when you will have to step in and help:

- They are making an error that would cause a major problem with equipment.

- They are performing the procedure incorrectly and it will affect what they do next.

- They are in danger of causing physical harm to themselves or others around them.

Mistakes that are not harmful may teach the trainees an important lesson. Just be certain that the lesson is not detrimental to the person or the process.

Take a Moment...

Think about how you will provide feedback to trainees during on-the-job training.

What should you consider when giving feedback to trainees?

_____

_____

What will you do to offer feedback in a positive way?

_____

_____

What will you do if you have to step in?

_____

_____

Help Trainees Gain Speed and Develop Accuracy

The first time trainees see you demonstrate a task at full speed it may be a blur to them. You make it look easy because you've done it before. Trainees are likely to be apprehensive about their ability to learn the task quickly. So put your efforts into helping them gain speed and develop accuracy. To do this you should:

- **Practice at a Slow Speed.** Allow trainees to work at their own pace at first. Have them increase their speed gradually until they can meet the time requirements for the job.

- **Focus on Techniques.** When trainees learn the proper techniques, they will develop speed as they continue to practice. It will be impossible for them to develop speed and gain accuracy until they sharpen the little things that are part of the bigger job.

- **Provide Tips From Experienced Employees.** Nearly every experienced employee has "tricks of the trade." Unless this is a new task which no one in the company has performed, share these tips with the trainees at the appropriate time in the training process. Some tips, if given too early, may confuse the trainees. Others, if given too late, will not be beneficial.

- **Establish Time Goals.** Trainees will develop speed sooner if they are given a deadline. Work with them to establish time goals for gaining speed and developing accuracy. Tell them when they should begin increasing their speed, and monitor their progress on a regular basis. Provide positive feedback as they come closer to reaching the goal.

6

"Provide positive feedback as they come closer to reaching the goal."

Take a Moment...

Think about how you will help trainees gain speed and develop accuracy during on-the-job training.

What specific techniques will you focus on to help trainees gain speed and develop accuracy?

_____

_____

_____

Which experienced employees can be involved in the training?

_____

_____

_____

What type of time goals are appropriate for the task?

_____

_____

_____

Chapter Six Review

Are the statements below True or False? Answers appear on page 98.

_____ 1. Tryout helps the trainer verify that learning has taken place.

_____ 2. Trainees should wait a couple of days after the presentation to do the tryout so the trainer can evaluate their ability to remember key facts.

_____ 3. Having trainees explain the task as they practice it helps to "program" them for doing it right in the future.

_____ 4. Multiple practices should be done by all trainees.

_____ 5. When observing the tryout, the trainer should look only at the end results achieved by the trainee.

_____ 6. Effective trainers give lots of feedback when trainees first begin to try out the task they are learning.

_____ 7. It's a good idea to give positive feedback even if the trainees make mistakes so they won't become discouraged.

_____ 8. Trainees may continue to make the same mistakes if the trainer focuses too much on their errors.

_____ 9. Most trainees who start out doing a job slowly never get any faster.

_____ 10. Using "tricks of the trade" should be avoided during on-the-job training.

Step Four - Follow-up

Chapter Objectives

After reading this chapter and completing the interactive exercises, you should be able to:

 Have the trainees work without supervision.

 Designate people who will help the trainees if they have questions.

 Reconfirm that trainees understand the task and are progressing in the workplace.

☑ Evaluate the effectiveness of your training procedures and content.

Importance of Training Follow-up

The follow-up process is the last, and very important, step in the four-step training method. It should be an on-going process after the trainee has completed the tryout. Follow-up should continue until the trainees understand the task and can do it correctly without additional training. It may continue for several hours, days, weeks, or even months, depending on the nature of the task.

The fourth step of the four-step training method is "follow-up."

During this step you will:
- Have Trainees Work Alone
- Designate "Helpers" for Trainees
- Reconfirm Trainees Understand Task
- Evaluate Training Procedures

Follow-up may occur in conjunction with the tryout, as shown in the sample customer service outline on page 13 in Chapter Three. In many cases, though, the trainees will work alone, without observation, after the tryout has been completed, and the trainer will conduct the follow-up later. When follow-up occurs later, it should be a two-way process in which the trainees contact the trainer for help, as needed, and the trainer checks to see how they are doing.

As another component of the follow-up, the trainer should measure the effectiveness of the training procedures to determine whether any changes are needed in the content before the next on-the-job training session is conducted. This includes a self-evaluation and requesting evaluations from trainees.

Have Trainees Work Alone

One of the best ways to build confidence in the trainees is to tell them you believe they are capable of working alone. Before you turn them loose, however, it's a good idea to review the task with them once again. Have them explain the key points and show you the correct way to perform the task. This also is a good opportunity to provide additional positive feedback, encourage them to continue to do the job right, and remind them about avoiding bad habits.

Don't back away completely from your trainees. The whole idea of follow-up is checking back after the trainees have been working alone for a while to see how they are doing. Check often, at first, as this is the time questions and problems will likely occur.

The follow-up covers many of the same activities as the tryout. When you check back, make it a point to observe employees performing the task and look for errors. Be prepared to provide feedback during the observation. Recognize their successes when they perform correctly. But don't ignore mistakes. If you find problems, correct mistakes in a supportive manner. Step in, when necessary, and provide assistance or retraining.

"One of the best ways to build confidence in the trainees is to tell them you believe they are capable of working alone."

7

Gradually reduce the frequency of your contacts with them. There are no hard-and-fast guidelines for when the process should be stopped. Each trainee is different. Some may require only one or two follow-up sessions, while others may need several sessions.

Take a Moment...

Think about your on-the-job training activity and what you will do when you have trainees work alone.

How will you decide when it's time to let the trainees work alone?

_____

_____

_____

What will you look for when you check back with the trainees after they have worked alone?

_____

_____

_____

How will you determine when the follow-up process should be stopped?

_____

_____

_____

Designate "Helpers" for Trainees

Before ending the follow-up, find "helpers" for the trainees. The trainees need someone who will be available to answer questions or solve problems. You may designate yourself, or you may decide to find another person.

Benefits of Designating Yourself

In most cases, you are the best person for the trainees to contact, since you have established a rapport with them.

- You know their strengths and weaknesses.
- You may take a more personal interest in the trainees.
- You are a "neutral" person who will provide answers to their training-related problems, assuming you are not the trainees' supervisor.
- You understand the task that the trainees are trying to incorporate in their jobs and will be able to provide them with solutions.

Benefits of Designating Others

There are situations when another person would be a better helper.

- You may not be available to help the trainees because you are training other employees or the demands on your time.
- Trainees may be reluctant to admit to you that they are experiencing problems.
- Trainees may prefer to go to their supervisor or another person in their work area.

7

What You Should Consider When Designating Others

If you decide to ask other people to assist the trainees as on-the-job helpers, be sure:

■ They have a good relationship with the employee, especially if the helper is a supervisor, as trainees may be intimidated by some people in authority.

■ They have the time and patience to work with trainees who are still learning a task and may make mistakes.

■ They have a thorough understanding of the task and are able to answer questions.

■ They have good people skills and can interact with the trainees without creating problems or having personality clashes.

When you designate someone else, give the helper direction in how to offer follow-up to the trainees. Provide a checklist of the areas to watch when working with the trainees. This may be a general checklist to which you add individualized comments about each trainee. Establish a procedure for what the helpers are expected to do after working with the trainees. Do the helpers tell you what they did? Do they tell the trainees' supervisor? Does the interaction remain confidential between the trainee and the designated person?

Take a Moment...

Think about your on-the-job training activity and designating "helpers" during the follow-up process.

Other than yourself, whom could you designate to help the trainee?

_____

_____

Can the employee's supervisor be used for follow-up? Why, or why not?

_____

_____

What direction will you provide for those who are going to help?

_____

_____

Reconfirm Trainees Understand the Task

The follow-up is the final opportunity to be sure the trainees understand exactly what they have to do and why. Depending on when the follow-up occurs and the nature of the task, you may not be able to see the trainee perform every part of the job. The process used during the follow-up step is essentially the same as the one used during the presentation/demonstration step.

7

"Your questions should ensure that the trainees understand the key concepts and give them confidence in their new skills."

Since you are not in the presentation/demonstration mode, you'll need to take a slightly different approach during follow-up than what is outlined in the method on page 27 in Chapter Three. As you are observing, ask, "Why is that a good way to do the job?" or "How were you trained to do that part of the task?" If they do not understand, review only the specific areas that you know are crucial to accomplishing the task correctly. Do not review the entire training program.

Avoid playing "Twenty Questions" with the trainees. You do not want to grill them; you are there to help. Your questions should ensure that the trainees understand the key concepts and give them confidence in their new skills. Your ability to evaluate accurately their understanding of the task will enable you to make the decision about when follow-up should be discontinued.

Take a Moment...

Think about the follow-up process and reconfirming that the trainees understand the task during on-the-job training.

What process will you use to ensure that the trainees understand the task?

_____

_____

What questions could you ask during follow-up?

_____

_____

What will you do if the trainee doesn't really understand?

_____

_____

Evaluate Training Procedures

Once the follow-up with the trainees has been completed, begin an evaluation of your training efforts. A thorough evaluation of your training procedures will uncover problems with any of the four steps of the process.

It's a good idea to involve your trainees in the evaluation, as they may have insights on areas you have not considered. Provide trainees with a questionnaire that can be completed easily, then returned to you. The questionnaire should be anonymous so trainees will feel free to express their opinions. If most of your training is one-on-one, you may want to wait until you have trained several people before sending out a questionnaire, so each trainee does not respond alone. Include questions that address each of the four steps of the training process. A sample questionnaire is found on page 94 in Chapter Nine.

In addition to asking for opinions on the questionnaire, you can include a few "test" questions patterned after the questions in the chapter reviews of this workbook. When reviewing the responses, compare the wrong answers with how many are right. Several people with wrong answers for the same question could indicate that either the question is faulty or information was not communicated clearly during the training. Don't get hung up on unusually high or low ratings by one or two trainees. Focus on the trends to get a true assessment of the training.

If you use a follow-up checklist for the trainees, you will have a record of the areas that cause problems frequently. Once again look for trends. Consider:

- Are many trainees making the same mistakes?
- Are there certain problem areas?
- What things are trainees doing well?
- Are trainees getting support from their helpers?

The answers to these questions will offer insight into the success of your training efforts.

Reviewing Yourself

After assessing the evaluations, take an objective review of yourself. This may be hard to do, but it is important. Ask these questions:

- Did I prepare the training content properly?
- Did I have the materials needed for the training?
- Did I ensure the training environment was conducive to learning?
- Was I open to questions from the trainees during each step?
- Was my presentation/demonstration effective?
- Did I take enough time to verify that the trainees understood the task?
- Did I have the trainees practice the task during a tryout?
- Did I have a follow-up after the training session?
- Does the trainee feel confident about performing the task?

Answers to these questions will indicate whether you need to make changes in your training before the next session. Compare your answers to the trainees' evaluations. Are your answers similar to those of the trainees? If not, which ones differ?

Filling out questionnaires takes valuable time away from the trainees' regular duties. Don't request an evaluation from the trainees unless you are prepared to do something with the results.

"Don't request an evaluation from the trainees unless you are prepared to do something with the results."

Take a Moment...

Think about how you can evaluate your training efforts.

How will you involve the trainees in your evaluation?

_____

_____

_____

What questions will you ask the trainees about your training efforts?

_____

_____

_____

What questions will you ask yourself?

_____

_____

_____

7

Chapter Seven Review

Complete the statements below. Suggested answers appear on page 98.

1. The follow-up process should continue until you are certain trainees can _____ the task without _____.

2. Follow-up should help your trainees build their _____.

3. List five things the trainer should do during initial stages of follow-up when the trainee is working alone.

    (1) _____

    (2) _____

    (3) _____

    (4) _____

    (5) _____

4. In most cases, the best person for the trainee to go to for help during the follow-up process is the _____.

5. If someone else helps the trainer with follow-up, it may be helpful to provide a _____ of things to look for.

6. The process used to reconfirm the trainees' understanding of the task is essentially the same as the process used during the _____ step.

7. A questionnaire sent to trainees to evaluate your training should be:

_____ A. Anonymous, so they are free to express their opinions

_____ B. Require trainees to put their names on them so you can talk to them if you have questions about their responses.

8. When reviewing evaluations, it's best to look for _____ in the responses.

9. A trainer should always do a _____ following every training session and compare it with the trainees' evaluations.

7

CHAPTER EIGHT

How to Handle Difficult Training Situations

Chapter Objectives

After reading this chapter, you should be able to handle the most common difficult training situations, including:

✓ What if the trainee falls back on old habits?

✓ What if the trainee still doesn't understand the task?

✓ What if you're stuck with a poor training environment?

✓ What if the trainee can't develop speed?

✓ What if the trainee doesn't take the training seriously?

✓ What if you don't have time to train?

Even If...

Even if you have an excellent training plan and follow the four-step method, you still may have situations that hinder your on-the-job training efforts. Following are six difficult training situations that will enable you to handle some of the most common training-related problems.

What If the Trainee Falls Back on Old Habits?

Effective training should change the trainee's behavior, as well as present and demonstrate the benefits of learning a new task. However, occasionally trainees who have some background in the task are resistant to change. They will have a tendency to fall back on what they already know and have trouble learning a new system because the task is "something like" what they've done previously.

You Should...

Try to find out if the trainees have experience with the task or have similar skills before beginning the training. During the training, you should explain what you want them to learn, how it is different from what they know, and why your approach is the one they have to use.

Address any questions or concerns they have about the new procedure. Always be sure they understand why the task must be performed a certain way. Don't allow old habits to continue or to surface during training. Present and demonstrate the "right way" and ensure that trainees know that continuing old habits is counterproductive for both the trainees and the organization.

What If the Trainee Still Doesn't Understand the Task?

You may think the trainees understand what you're telling them because they nod their heads frequently in an affirmative manner. Then, when it's time for them to practice the task, it is obvious they don't know what to do. This can lead to feelings of frustration for the trainees and for you. If you allow this frustration to show, it can damage your relationship with the trainees.

"Always be sure they understand why the task must be performed a certain way."

You Should...

Accept the responsibility for helping the trainee learn the task. It's been said that if the trainee hasn't learned, the trainer hasn't taught. When you finish the training and find the trainee doesn't understand, reverse the training process.

Begin by going through the steps in a "reverse mode" from the way in which they were presented originally. At each point, verify that the trainees grasp what is being taught before you move forward again. If the trainee does not understand, take a short break. In certain situations, you should consider rescheduling the training. If this occurs, talk with the trainee's supervisor. The trainee may not be suited for the task. In that case, recommend that the trainee stop the training.

Before you make this decision, there are preventive measures for this situation.

- Ask questions to verify the trainee really does know what you're saying and isn't just nodding in agreement to please you or to avoid the embarrassment of not understanding.

- Involve the trainee in the presentation of the task.

- Have the trainee practice the task earlier in the training rather than in the tryout.

- Ask the trainee's opinion about how the training would be helpful on the job.

If you decide to discontinue the training, be sure to communicate the reason to the trainee in a supportive way. Emphasize that the trainee may be better-suited for another task.

What If You're Stuck With a Poor Training Environment?

Trainers have to be resourceful. Many training environments are less than ideal, especially when conducting on-the-job training. Dim lighting conditions, noisy surroundings, and people trying to perform their jobs can be distractions when you are trying to train.

You Should...

Consider conducting the training in a different place. Do you have to be "on the job?" Could you move out of the distracting environment and simulate the workplace in a neutral space without too much expense?

Also consider conducting the training at a different time. Are there "slow" periods during the day that would make it easier for trainees to focus on the training? Can the training be postponed? The training could be offered before or after regular work hours when there will be less confusion and less concern that trainees are "missing work."

Can you get someone to assist you? If you are training a group, another person may be able to train part of the group so you don't have too many people in one place at one time. Employees who have completed the training successfully could assist. And they would be good examples for the trainees.

8

What If the Trainee Can't Develop Speed?

It's important that you perform the task at the required speed during the demonstration. This makes the trainees aware of the standards.

Most trainees will try to develop speed before they understand the process involved in performing the task correctly. However, you may have a trainee who just can't develop the necessary speed. This can become frustrating to the trainee, the trainer, and other employees.

You Should...

Slow down your demonstration so the trainee can see the task performed correctly. Perhaps it was too fast for the trainee. Also, be sure the trainee has the opportunity to practice the task in a controlled environment. Don't throw the trainees into "live" situations before they are ready.

When the trainee performs the task correctly, set time goals for achieving the desired productivity and, together, measure the trainee's progress against the goals. A trainee who cannot achieve the desired speed after a reasonable amount of time may not be physically capable of achieving the standards for the task. In this case the trainee may have to be terminated or transferred. Before you recommend this "final" action, speak with the trainee's supervisor and explain the situation to be certain you have done everything you can to help the trainee be successful.

What If the Trainee Doesn't Take the Training Seriously?

Sometimes people are scheduled for training but are not told why they require the training. Other times trainees do not think they need training. If trainees don't see the value in training, they can become disruptive in a group session. In a one-on-one situation, they may appear bored, uninterested, or even antagonistic. As long as they are unreceptive, you will have trouble teaching a new skill or process to them.

You Should...

Find out whether the trainees know why they were sent to training. Do this in a private conversation. Don't confront or embarrass them in the presence of others. If the trainees do not know why they are in the session, review the learning objectives with them and compare these objectives to what they know about the task.

Even after you've done this, the trainees still may not agree that they require training. Before continuing, contact their supervisor and ask why they were scheduled. Should the response not seem valid, suggest an alternative to the training.

8

What If You Don't Have Time to Train?

Training does take time. There's no way of getting around that. You need time to prepare, time to present and demonstrate, time to have the trainees try out the task, and time for the follow-up. By leaving out one of these steps, you'll reduce, or possibly eliminate, the value of the training. If you really don't have time to do it properly, you may have to cancel the training. Before you take that action, consider some of the following ideas.

You Should...

Admit that you need help and find other people to assist you with the training. Look for employees who have the "helper" qualities described on page 68 in Chapter Seven and ask them to help. You'll be surprised how many people will say, "Yes."

Once you have selected your helpers, give them the information and materials required for the training session. (You could start by having them read this book!) Then acquaint them with the specifics of the task they'll be training.

Next, decide whether you want the helpers to be involved in the whole training process or just selected parts. Some trainers prefer to do the presentation and demonstration themselves and then turn over the trainees to the assistants for the tryout and follow-up. This approach makes it easier to find people to be helpers since they don't have to do a presentation and demonstration.

If this sounds as though it's going to take time, you're right—at least in the beginning. In the long run, however, you'll save time by having this extra help.

Chapter Eight Review

Indicate whether the statements below are True or False. Answers appear on page 98.

_____ 1. If trainees have trouble developing the required speed to perform a task, it could be because the trainer's demonstration was too fast.

_____ 2. Putting trainees in a "live" situation early on in the training can help them develop the necessary speed.

_____ 3. Trainees may not take training seriously if they do not know why they have been sent to training.

_____ 4. If there is no valid reason for a person being in the training, you should allow them to stay just in case they might learn something useful.

_____ 5. Trainees may fall back on old habits if they have similar skills or have learned to perform the task you are teaching in a different way.

_____ 6. One solution to a poor training environment may be to conduct the training at a different time.

_____ 7. Using a simulated environment for training should only be considered as a last resort.

_____ 8. Finding "helpers" can solve the dilemma of not having enough time to train.

_____ 9. A helper can be assigned to teach any part of the training.

_____ 10. A trainee who does not understand the task after you explain it probably has a bad attitude.

CHAPTER NINE

Tools for Implementing On-the-Job Training and Evaluation

Chapter Objectives

After reading this chapter and completing the interactive exercises, you should be able to:

☑ Assess your readiness to implement on-the-job training.

☑ Develop a plan for implementing on-the-job training.

Are You Ready?

By now you have a good idea about how to use the four-step training method to meet your on-the-job training needs. Perhaps you still have a few questions about how you implement the training plan.

The self-assessment that follows will enable you to determine where you are in the implementation process and to identify areas that need to be reworked before you begin training. In addition to the assessment exercise, you'll find other tools in this chapter that will guide you in putting your plan into action for successful on-the-job training.

Self-Assessment for Implementing On-the-Job Training

The key principles of on-the-job training are summarized below. Evaluate your readiness to apply these principles to your training by rating yourself according to the scale below. Refer to the chapters listed in the parentheses for review in these areas. Also, use the tools following this self-assessment for more help.

Use the following scale to rate each statement:

5–Strongly Agree   4–Agree   3–Not Sure   2–Disagree   1–Strongly Disagree

_____ I can describe the two purposes of training. **(Chapter One)**

_____ I can explain the benefits of training. **(Chapter One)**

_____ I can describe the four-step training method. **(Chapter Three)**

_____ I can define when the four-step method should be used. **(Chapter Three)**

_____ I have specific criteria to use when selecting trainers. **(Chapter Three)**

_____ I can write specific, measurable, realistic, and observable learning objectives. **(Chapter Two)**

_____ I can use the whole-part-whole approach when developing a training plan. **(Chapter Two)**

_____ I am able to prepare myself and my employees for training. **(Chapters Four and Eight)**

_____ I am able to prepare training materials and the training environment. **(Chapters Four and Eight)**

9

_____ I am able to make an effective presentation for on-the-job training. **(Chapter Five)**

_____ I can apply the techniques needed to demonstrate a task properly to trainees. **(Chapter Five)**

_____ I have at least two ways to verify that trainees understand the task. **(Chapter Five)**

_____ I have a definite plan for having trainees practice a new task during the tryout. **(Chapter Six)**

_____ I can reinforce positive actions by trainees through feedback. **(Chapter Six)**

_____ I can help trainees develop speed when learning a new task. **(Chapters Six and Eight)**

_____ I have a plan for doing follow-up. **(Chapter Seven)**

_____ I can evaluate the effectiveness of my training. **(Chapter Seven)**

Review each of your responses again. A rating of 3 or below indicates an area requiring improvement before you implement on-the-job training. You also should determine whether there are ways to move your 4s to 5s.

Writing Learning Objectives

As we discussed in Chapter Two on page 16, good learning objectives are defined in terms of "doing words" to identify what the learner will be able to do after training. Here are some more descriptive terms you can use when writing learning objectives. Practice writing a few more sample learning objectives below.

identify	define	distinguish
sort	prioritize	alter
load	connect	transfer
select	list	describe
explain	calculate	compare
guide	monitor	convert
assign	find	mark
arrange	total	complete

Sample Learning Objectives:

_____

_____

_____

_____

_____

9

Template for Preparing a Training Outline

This template should be used whenever you are developing an on-the-job training plan.

Training Outline Template

I. Preparation

A. After training, the participant(s) will be able to:

_____

_____

_____

B. I will prepare myself physically and mentally by:

_____

_____

_____

C. I will need the following materials:

_____

_____

_____

D. I will prepare the training environment by:

_____

_____

_____

E. I will prepare the trainee(s) by:

_____

_____

_____

II. Presentation/Demonstration Outline

(Define your learning objectives using the whole-part-whole approach. Each objective should have a separate outline.)

_____

_____

_____

_____

_____

_____

_____

_____

_____

III. Tryout

I will have the trainee(s) practice each of these tasks:

_____

_____

_____

_____

_____

_____

_____

_____

9

During tryout I will:

_____

_____

_____

_____

_____

_____

IV. Follow-up

If there are problems, trainee(s) should contact:

_____

_____

_____

_____

I will check back every _____ hours for _____ days, _____ weeks, _____months.

I will evaluate the effectiveness of my training efforts by:

_____

_____

_____

_____

_____

Examples of Tryout and Follow-up Checklists

Experienced trainers take different approaches to the tryout and follow-up steps. Some keep the two steps separate, while others prefer to combine them. Trainers also have combined the tryout with the presentation and demonstration. You should decide which method will work best for you. That decision may be determined by the task being trained.

Example 1: Combined Presentation/ Demonstration and Tryout

Directions: Check the space provided when presentation and demonstration are completed and the trainee practices the task.

Task: Safety

- Why safety is important
- Use proper lifting procedures
- Wear proper safety gear
- Wear eye protection at all times
- Safe handling of hazardous materials
- Read material safety data sheets

_____ Presentation/Demonstration and Tryout have been completed.

Date Completed: _____

9

Example 2: Combined Tryout and Follow-Up

Directions: Check the space provided when the trainee practices the task and when you finish the follow-up.

Task: Safety

	Tryout	Follow-Up
■ Why safety is important	_____	_____
■ Use proper lifting procedures	_____	_____
■ Wear proper safety gear	_____	_____
■ Wear eye protection at all times	_____	_____
■ Safe handling of hazardous materials	_____	_____
■ Read material safety data sheets	_____	_____

Date Completed: _____

Example 3: Separate Tryout and Follow-up

Tryout

Check the space provided when the trainee practices each task listed below.

Task: Safety

■ Why safety is important	_____
■ Use proper lifting procedures	_____
■ Wear proper safety gear	_____
■ Wear eye protection at all times	_____
■ Safe handling of hazardous materials	_____
■ Read material safety data sheets	_____

Follow-up

When the trainee has met the safety standards, the trainer and trainee should sign a statement such as the one below.

The signatures below indicate that the trainee has satisfactorily completed the training outlined above according to standards established by the trainer and the company.

_____   _____

Employee Signature   *Date*

_____   _____

Trainer Signature   *Date*

Sample Form for Trainees' Evaluation of Training Session

Use the form below to get feedback from the trainees about your on-the-job training.

Trainee's Evaluation

Training Session Attended: _____

Use the following scale to rate each statement:

5–Strongly Agree   4–Agree   3–Not Sure   2–Disagree   1–Strongly Disagree

_____ The trainer was prepared.

_____ The material was well-organized.

_____ The handouts were helpful.

_____ The trainer had a thorough knowledge of the subject.

_____ The trainer explained and demonstrated the task so it was easy to understand.

_____ The trainer allowed enough time for questions after each step.

_____ The trainer maintained my interest.

_____ I was given a chance to practice the task in a non-threatening atmosphere.

_____ Someone was available to answer questions after training.

_____ I learned to perform the task properly.

Did you find the training valuable? Why or why not?

_____

_____

_____

_____

What suggestions do you have for improving the training?

_____

_____

_____

_____

9

Answers to Chapter Exercises

Chapter One

Statements 1, 5 , 6, and 8 are **False.** Statements 2, 3, and 7 are **True.**

Chapter Two

1. (1) Realistic
    (2) Observable
    (3) Measurable
    (4) Specific

2. Increase sales in 1996 by 5 percent over 1995.

3. Job-related and audio-visual

4. The first, second, and fourth statements are **True.**

5. **Whole** – Tell them what you're going to tell them
    Part – Tell them
    Whole – Tell them what you told them

6. False

7. The second and third reasons are **True.**

8. False

Chapter Three

1. II. Presentation/Demonstration
   III. Tryout

2. Here are four:
   (1) It's easy to use.
   (2) It can be used on-the-job.
   (3) You don't have to be a training expert to use it.
   (4) You can develop your own outline.

3. time restraints
   line management training responsibility
   workplace flexibility
   cost considerations
   realistic setting

4. Any five of the following are acceptable:
   good communication skills
   knowledge of the subject
   on-the-job experience
   patience
   interest in helping people learn
   respect of others
   sense of humor

5. first or initial

6. positive focus

Chapter Four

Statements 3 ,4 , and 9 are **False.** Statements 1, 2, 5, 6, 7, and 8 are **True.**

Chapter Five

1. show and tell

2. learning objectives

3. logical

4. jargon and buzz words

5. 3 to 5

Chapter Five (Cont.)

6. beside the trainer

7. expected

8. "Yes" or "No"

9. responsibility

10. False

11. False

Chapter Six

Statements 2, 5, 7, 9, and 10 are **False**. Statements 1, 3, 4, 6, and 8 are **True**.

Chapter Seven

1. perform additional training

2. confidence

3. (1) Observe
   (2) Provide feedback
   (3) Recognize their successes
   (4) Correct mistakes in a supportive manner
   (5) Step in, when necessary

4. trainer

5. checklist

6. presentation/demonstration

7. A

8. trends

9. self-evaluation

Chapter Eight

Statements 2, 4, 7, and 10 are **False**. Statements 1, 3, 5, 6, 8, and 9 are **True.**

Additional Resources

Books

Broadwell, Martin M. *The Supervisor as an Instructor.* Reading, Massachusetts: Addison-Wesley Publishing Company, Inc., 1984.

Buckley, Roger and Jim Caple. *One-to-One Training and Coaching Skills.* San Diego, California: Pfeiffer & Company, 1991.

Mager, Robert F. *What Every Manager Should Know About Training.* Belmont, California: Lake Publishing Company, 1992.

Nilson, Carolyn. *Training for Non-Trainers.* New York: AMACOM, 1990.

Wexley, Kenneth M. and Gary P. Latham. *Developing and Training Human Resources in Organizations.* New York: HarperCollins Publishers, Inc., 1991.

Zaccarelli, Brother Herman E., C.S.C. *Training Managers to Train.* Los Altos, California: Crisp Publications, Inc., 1988.

Audio-Cassette/Workbook Program

Cadwell, Charles M. *Developing an Employee Orientation and Training Program.* New York: American Management Association, 1990.

Additional Resources
from American Media Incorporated

Other AMI How-to Series Books

Assertiveness Skills

Customer Service Excellence

Documenting Discipline

Effective Delegation Skills

Effective Teamwork Skills

High Impact Presentations

The Human Touch Performance Appraisal

I Have to Fire Someone!

Interviewing: More Than a Gut Feeling

Investing Time for Maximum Return

Listen Up: Hear What's Really Being Said

Making Change Work for You!

Making Meetings Work

Managing Conflict at Work

Managing Stress

The New Supervisor: Skills for Success

Positive Mental Attitude and the Workplace

Self-Esteem: The Power to Be Your Best

Ten Tools for Quality

Other Products Available on These Subjects

Americans with Disabilities Act • AIDS Awareness • Banking • Business Writing • Change • Communication • Computer PC Training • Conflict Resolution • Creative Problem Solving • Cultural Diversity • Customer Service • Empowerment • Ethics • Family and Medical Leave Act • Healthcare Employee Training • Healthcare Safety • Icebreaker • Interviewing • Listening Skills • Motivation • Outplacement • Paradigms • Performance Appraisal • Professional Image • Quality • Retail • Safety • Sales Training • Sexual Harassment • Stress • Substance Abuse • Supervision • Teamwork • Telephone Skills • Time Management • And Many More!

**To order additional American Media Incorporated resources, call
(800) 262-2557**

NOTES

NOTES

NOTES

NOTES